Get Your Hands on Problem Solving

grade 3

**Look for a Pattern • Make a Picture • Use Logical Thinking
Make an Organized List • Guess and Check
Make a Table • Act Out With Objects**

BASED ON NCTM STANDARDS

by Shirley Hoogeboom & Judy Goodnow

Get Your Hands on Problem Solving, Grade 3

Limited Reproduction Permission: Permission to duplicate these materials is limited to the teacher for whom they are purchased. Reproduction for an entire school or school district is unlawful and strictly prohibited.

Shirley Hoogeboom and Judy Goodnow are authors, curriculum developers, and editors for Ideal School Supply Company. Together they have taught children at the kindergarten level through grade six. As curriculum developers, they have each authored or coauthored over 100 books and sets of games and activities for reading, language arts, and math. They have conducted workshops for teachers in the use of math manipulatives and computer-related materials.

Shirley holds a bachelor of arts degree in Education from Calvin College where she earned her Michigan Teaching Credential. She completed further studies in education at the University of Minnesota and earned her California Teaching Credential at California State University, Hayward.

Judy holds a bachelor of arts degree from Wellesley College, a master's degree in Interactive Educational Technology from Stanford University, and earned her California Teaching Credential at San Jose State University.

Art Director: Nancy Tseng
Cover Design: Lee McCoy Creative Center
Illustrations: Duane Bibby
Text Design and Production: London Road Design, Redwood City, CA

ISBN: 1-56451-256-8
Get Your Hands on Problem Solving, Grade 3
© 1998 Ideal School Supply
A Division of Instructional Fair Group, Inc.
A Tribune Education Company
3195 Wilson Drive NW, Grand Rapids, MI 49544 • USA
Duke Street, Wisbech, Cambs, PE13 2AE • UK
All Rights Reserved • Printed in USA

Table of Contents

Notes to the Teacher	iv
Four-Step Plan for Problem Solving	vii
Problem-Solving Strategies	viii
Cross-Reference Chart	x
Assessment Ideas	xi
Children's Books as Resources for Creating Problems	xii
Blackline Master for Play Money and Number Tiles	xiii
Blackline Master for Recording Sheet	xiv
Solutions	xv
Teaching Plan for Story Problem 1: **Look for a Pattern, Act Out With Objects**	1
Teaching Plan for Story Problem 2: **Look for a Pattern, Act Out With Objects**	2
Story Problems 1–6	3
Teaching Plan for Story Problem 7: **Make a Picture or Diagram, Act Out With Objects**	9
Teaching Plan for Story Problem 8: **Make a Picture or Diagram, Act Out With Objects**	10
Story Problems 7–12	11
Teaching Plan for Story Problem 13: **Use Logical Thinking**	17
Teaching Plan for Story Problem 14: **Use Logical Thinking**	18
Story Problems 13–18	19
Teaching Plan for Story Problem 19: **Guess and Check, Act Out With Objects**	25
Teaching Plan for Story Problem 20: **Guess and Check, Act Out With Objects**	26
Story Problems 19–24	27
Teaching Plan for Story Problem 25: **Make a Table, Act Out With Objects**	33
Teaching Plan for Story Problem 26: **Make a Table, Act Out With Objects**	34
Story Problems 25–30	35
Teaching Plan for Story Problem 31: **Make an Organized List, Act Out With Objects**	41
Teaching Plan for Story Problem 32: **Make an Organized List, Act Out With Objects**	42
Story Problems 31–36	43
Practice Story Problems 37–68	49

Notes to the Teacher

This is the third in a series of books designed to help students become confident problem solvers:

Get Your Hands on Problem Solving, Grade 1
Get Your Hands on Problem Solving, Grade 2
Get Your Hands on Problem Solving, Grade 3

The activities in this series introduce students to nonroutine logic and math story problems, plus a four-step plan and seven strategies for solving them. One of the strategies—Act Out With Objects—is often used in combination with the other strategies: Look for a Pattern, Make a Picture or Diagram, Use Logical Thinking, Guess and Check, Make a Table, and Make an Organized List.

These strategies are tools that students can use for solving a variety of problems. The activities in this book help students develop a sense of which strategies will be most useful for solving given problems. Learning to use the strategies helps students build confidence in their ability to solve problems.

The National Council of Teachers of Mathematics (NCTM) stresses that "Problem solving should be the central focus of the mathematics curriculum. . . . Ideally, students should share their thinking and approaches with other students and with teachers, and they should learn several ways of representing problems and strategies for solving them. In addition, they should learn to value the process of solving problems as much as they value the solutions. . . . A major goal of problem-solving instruction is to enable children to develop and apply strategies to solve problems."

Contents
This book presents logic and math story problems at a simple level. The stories often show humorous characters in situations that are familiar to children.

There are six sections of story problems that can be used to introduce the problem-solving process and strategies. Each section includes six story problem activity sheets, plus teaching plans for the first two story problems. The teaching plans give sample teacher-and-student dialogs that model the problem-solving process and the use of the strategy being introduced. Some also suggest that students act out the problem with objects.

Examples:

Teaching Plan

Story Problem Activity Sheet

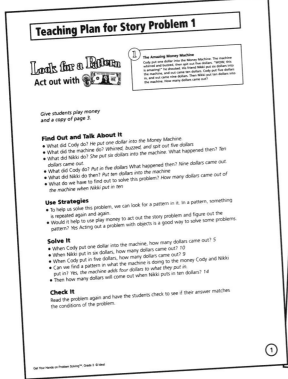
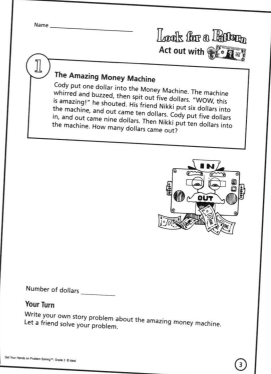

In each section, the first and second problems and teaching plans introduce the children to two different types of problems that they can solve with the same strategy. There is one more problem of each type within the section, plus two more of a third type that can be solved using the same strategy.

The story problem activity sheets name the strategy or strategies being introduced, and, when appropriate, show a picture of the objects students can use to act out the problem. They give one story problem, plus a Doing More or Your Turn activity for the students to do after they have solved the story problem. The Doing More activities are extensions of the problem, and the Your Turn activities encourage children to create their own problems for their peers to solve.

There are 32 practice story problems on pages 49–64, which can be used for assessment and/or for additional practice. Students will be able to choose the strategy or strategies they think will be most helpful for solving the problem. You can give students a copy of the Recording Sheet on page xiv if you wish to have them show their work and what strategies they used.

The objects suggested for the story problems in this book are play coins and bills; number tiles 0 through 9; and colored cubes or squares of paper.

Linking Cubes (ID7617), One-Inch Colored Cubes (ID3604), Overhead Numeral Tiles (ID7246), Plastic Coins (ID7509), and Toy Bills (ID7502) are available from Ideal or any Ideal dealer. A blackline master for paper number tiles, coins, and bills is provided on page xiii.

The Four-Step Plan and Problem-Solving Strategies that will be used for solving the story problems are explained on pages vii–ix.

In the Cross-Reference Chart on page x, a strategy is suggested for each problem. However, students should be encouraged to use whatever strategy they find most helpful, including ones that they devise themselves.

Assessment Ideas are given on page xi, and Solutions are provided on pages xv–xvi. If you wish to create more problems similar to those included in this book, the children's books listed on page xii may provide a rich resource for familiar characters and contexts.

Teaching Suggestions

It is recommended that students work together in pairs. This kind of grouping allows children to talk together about what they are thinking and how they are solving the problems.

Give each student a copy of the story problem activity sheet, and a supply of cubes, number tiles, or play money if any are suggested.

Begin by reading the story problem with the students. Some children may need to hear it several times to retain the information. Invite the students to restate the problem in their own words.

Then guide the students through the problem-solving process, following the teaching plan or your own plan for that story problem. (In the teaching plans provided, the dialogs include sample questions you might ask, and, in italics, some possible answers students might give.) Begin by asking questions to help the students find all of the information in the problem that they will need to solve it. Next, talk about the strategies, or tools, that can be used to solve the problem. Help the children use the strategies, and encourage them to talk about their thinking as they solve the problem. At this stage, the development of math language and reasoning is more important than getting the right answer. The students may even discover their own unique ways of solving the problem that they will use again and again. They are building a library of ways to think about and solve problems, and at the same time are building confidence in themselves as problem solvers.

You may want to have the students record their answers as suggested on the activity sheet. After the students have solved a story problem, reread the story while they check to see that their solutions meet all the conditions given in the problem.

A Four-Step Plan for Problem Solving

Step one is to **FIND OUT AND TALK ABOUT IT.** In this beginning step, students find out what the problem means and what question must be answered to solve it. It is important that children know the meaning of all the words used in the story problem and understand what is going on in the problem. They should also learn how to find each piece of important information.

Step two is to choose and **USE STRATEGIES.** In this step, students begin to think about the tools they can use to solve the problem and which tools will be most helpful.

Step three is to **SOLVE IT.** In this step, students use the strategy and any objects suggested to find a solution to the problem. On many of the student activity pages, pictures or tables or organized lists have been started to introduce the strategy to the children. Help the students complete them and use them to solve the problem. The children can also record their solutions in the ways suggested on the student pages.

Step four is to **CHECK IT.** In this step, the students should reread the problems and review their work and solution. They need to make sure their solution fits with the clues and information given in the problem.

Problem-Solving Strategies

Act Out With Objects • Students will use cubes, number tiles, and play coins and bills to act out many of the story problems in this book. Being able to act out the story with these objects helps students visualize what is going on in the problem, understand the underlying math concepts, and work out the solution.

Look for a Pattern • A pattern is a regular, systematic repetition. Identifying the pattern helps the problem solver predict what will "come next." In story problems 1 through 6, children will identify and continue a variety of number patterns.

Make a Picture • Making pictures or diagrams, such as number lines and Venn circle diagrams, can be very useful for solving some problems. In story problems 7 through 12, students will be completing Venn diagrams, diagrams divided into fractional parts, and pictures representing streets and rivers (a type of number line) or other map-like drawings to solve the problems.

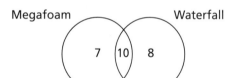 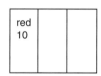

Use Logical Thinking • Logical reasoning is really used in all problem solving. Logical thinking is especially needed, however, for the types of problems that include or imply conditional statements such as "If . . . then," or "If . . . then . . . else." Story problems 13 through 18 give some clues, and the students will use "If . . . then" kind of thinking to fill in missing information and solve the problems.

	apple	raisins	popsicle	chocolate chip cookie
Juan	yes	no	no	no
Rodney	no			no
Maria	no	no	no	yes
Joan	no			no

Guess and Check • In some story problems, information is given in an indirect way. Students have to make a guess for one number, or a sum of numbers, in order to work out the problem. Then they check to see if the solution is correct. If not, they use the information from the incorrect guess to make another more informed guess. Students use this strategy to solve story problems 19 through 24.

>   guess: 3 blue, 6 red, 1 yellow, 3 + 6 + 1 = 10, too low
>   guess: 5 blue, 8 red, 3 yellow, 5 + 8 + 3 = 16, OK

Make a Table • Problem solvers find that making tables helps them organize and keep track of information, discover missing information, and identify data that is asked for in the problem. The recording spaces for story problems 25 through 30 show the beginnings of tables. Problem solvers will find that tables can be made in many different forms; for example, T-charts, vertical tables, and horizontal tables.

Groups	Students	Grandparents	Total People
1	4	1	5
2	8	2	10
3	12	3	15

Make an Organized List • Making an organized list helps students organize and keep track of their work with the data. This kind of step-by-step approach to solving the problem makes it easier for the problem solver to review what steps have been taken and pinpoint what steps still need to be completed. An organized approach is particularly helpful when a problem solver needs to find ALL of the possible solutions; for example, all the ways that a group of colored objects can be combined in groups of four or five, or that coins can be combined to make a given amount of money. The recording spaces for story problems 31 through 36 show the beginnings of organized lists.

Groups of Coins Worth 65¢

Quarters	Dimes	Nickels	Coins in all
2	1	1	4
2	0	3	5

Cross-Reference Chart

Teaching Story Problems	**Strategies and Manipulatives**
1	Look for a Pattern, Act Out With Objects (play money)
2, 3, 4, 5, 6	Look for a Pattern, Act Out With Objects (cubes)
7, 8, 10, 11	Make a Picture or Diagram, Act Out With Objects (cubes)
9, 12	Make a Picture or Diagram
13, 14, 15, 16, 17, 18	Use Logical Thinking
19, 22	Guess and Check, Act Out With Objects (cubes)
20, 23	Guess and Check, Act Out With Objects (number tiles)
22, 24	Guess and Check, Act Out With Objects (play money)
25, 27, 28, 29	Make a Table, Act Out With Objects (cubes)
26, 30	Make a Table, Act Out With Objects (play money)
31, 32, 34, 35	Make an Organized List, Act Out With Objects (play money)
33, 36	Make an Organized List, Act Out With Objects (cubes)

Practice Story Problems	**Strategies and Manipulatives***
38	Look for a Pattern, Act Out With Objects (play money)
53	Look for a Pattern, Act Out With Objects (cubes)
47, 57	Look for a Pattern
37, 45, 63, 68	Make a Picture or Diagram, Act Out With Objects (cubes)
55	Make a Picture or Diagram
46, 49, 60, 66	Use Logical Thinking
39, 43	Guess and Check, Act Out With Objects (cubes)
51, 56	Guess and Check, Act Out With Objects (number tiles)
61, 65	Guess and Check, Act Out With Objects (play money)
40, 48, 52, 59, 67	Make a Table, Act Out With Objects (cubes)
64	Make a Table, Act Out With Objects (play money)
41, 44, 50, 54	Make an Organized List, Act Out With Objects (play money)
58	Make an Organized List, Act Out With Objects (cubes)
62	Make an Organized List, Act Out With Objects (number tiles)

* The strategies and manipulatives shown can be used for solving the practice problems; however, children may choose to use other strategies and solve the problems without the use of manipulatives.

Assessment Ideas

These problems provide an excellent opportunity for assessing your students' reasoning skills and mathematical understanding. You can use any of the problems as an informal assessment tool or in combination with the simple scoring rubric shown below. You may prefer to use a scoring rubric that is part of your school district's curriculum, if that is available. Different numbers of levels are possible in a scoring rubric; we have shown only three.

With these problem-solving activities, it is more important to evaluate the students' reasoning skills and mathematical thinking than to concentrate on arithmetic or computation skills. Allow for computational errors, if a student shows an understanding of how to use a problem-solving strategy and has provided sound reasoning for how to solve the problem.

For informal assessment, you can record observations of the students as they work together to solve a problem. As you make your observations, you will want to concentrate on how the students communicate with one another: Do they contribute ideas, question ideas, show initiative, explain their thinking? Also note how they work with a partner or group: Do they build on ideas, exchange ideas, listen to ideas, work cooperatively? Also observe how they use the manipulatives: Do they use them in appropriate ways, revealing an understanding of the problem?

Here is a simple scoring rubric that you can use:

Needs Improvement
Does not understand the problem question
Cannot extract relevant information from the problem
Does not communicate clear thinking
Makes major errors

Good
Seems to understand the problem question
Extracts some relevant information from the problem
Shows an attempt to work out the problem
Communicates thinking, but not adequate mathematical reasoning

Very Good
Understands the problem question
Extracts relevant information from the problem
Communicates thinking clearly
Demonstrates mathematical thinking
Provides a complete solution which shows understanding of the problem-solving process

Children's Books as Resources for Creating Problems

Children's literature offers a wealth of characters and settings for creating story problems similar to the ones in this book. Imagine the delight of students when they discover their favorite storybook characters in the problems! This gives the students greater incentive for solving the problems, and helps them connect mathematics with literature. They may even use your story problems as models for creating their own storybook problems.

The following children's books are just a few of the many that can be used as resources for problems. Most of them can be used for more than one strategy. You can also use favorite characters from the books your students are reading and from familiar folktales.

Look for a Pattern
King Henry's Palace, by Pat Hutchins
Commander Toad and the Space Pirates, by Jane Yolen

Make a Picture or Diagram
Elves Don't Wear Hard Hats (The Bailey Shool Kids), by Debbie Dadey and Marcia Thornton Jones
The Littles Go Exploring, by John Peterson

Guess and Check
The Littles, by John Peterson
Schoolhouse Mystery (The Boxcar Children), by Gertrude Chandler Warner

Make a Table
A Cricket in Times Square, by George Selden
Charlotte's Web by E. B. White

Use Logical Thinking
Mr. Popper's Penguins, by Richard and Florence Atwater
Zombies Don't Play Soccer (The Bailey School Kids), by Richard and Florence Atwater
A Three Hat Day, by Laura Geringer

Make an Organized List
Charlie and the Chocolate Factory, by Roald Dahl
The Littles Take a Trip, by John Peterson

Here is one example of a story problem using characters and a setting from *Mr. Popper's Penguins:*

> The Penguins lined up behind Mr. Popper, and they all marched grandly onto the stage. Victoria was right behind Mr. Popper. Isabella was behind Scott. Adelina was between Nelson and Scott, and Captain Cook was last in line. Where was each penguin in the line?

Get Your Hands on Problem Solving, Grade 3 © Ideal

Play Money and Number Tiles

0	1	2	3	4	5	6	7	8	9
0	1	2	3	4	5	6	7	8	9

Recording Sheet

Name _____ Problem Number _____

Show your work and solution.

Act Out With 🂠	Look for a Pattern	Guess and Check
Act Out With	Use Logical Thinking	Make a Table
Act Out With	Make a Picture or Diagram	Make an Organized List

Get Your Hands on Problem Solving, Grade 3 © Ideal

Solutions

Story Problem

1. $14
2. Friday

   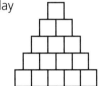

   Doing More: Saturday

3. 21

   Doing More: 6th minute
4. 18
5. 5; 🐭🐭🐭🐭
6. 96

   Doing More: 11
7. 25

   Doing More: 27
8. 6 green, 12 total

   Doing More: 9 green, 18 total
9. 14 blocks long
10. 47

    Doing More: 58
11. 30

    Doing More: 33
12. 9 miles long

    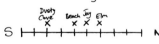
13. 4 pounds

    Doing More: 2 pounds
14. Juan—apple, Rodney—popsicle, Maria—chocolate chip cookie, Joan—raisins
15. Rabbit, Frog, Cat, Rabbit, Bird or, Rabbit, Cat, Frog, Rabbit, Bird
16. $18

    Doing More: $24
17. Tyrone—swim, Ray—soccer, Jamila—tennis, Sandy—bike
18. Bear, Rabbit, Owl, Rabbit, Bear, Chipmunk

    Doing More: Owl, Frog, Frog, Bear, Chipmunk, Bear
19. 8 red, 5 blue, 3 yellow

    Doing More: 10 red, 8 blue, 4 yellow
20. | 3 | 8 | 1 |
    |---|---|---|
    | 7 | | 5 |
    | 2 | 4 | 6 |

    Other solutions are possible.

    Doing More:

21. 18 pennies, 6 nickels, 3 dimes

    Doing More: 1 penny, 2 nickels, 2 quarters
22. 3 blue, 3 green, 5 white, 2 orange
23. | 9 | 4 | 3 |
    |---|---|---|
    | 5 | | 7 |
    | 2 | 8 | 6 |

    Other solutions are possible.

    Doing More:

7	2	9
3		5
8	6	4

    Other solutions are possible.
24. 2 quarters, 8 dimes, 3 nickels

    Doing More: 4 quarters, 12 dimes, 8 nickels
25. 7 kittens, 21 dogs

    Doing More: 14 kittens, 28 dogs
26. 7

    Doing More: 8 weeks
27. 7 grandparents, 28 students

    Doing More: 10 grandparents, 40 students
28. 30 pig hats, 42 goat hats
29. 15 caterpillums, 30 smuzzywompers

    Doing More: 8 ketchopias, 24 picklefobs
30. 10

    Doing More: 15 weeks
31. 3 nickels, 5 pennies

    Doing More: 2 nickels, 10 pennies
32. 6 stegosaurus, 2 tricerotops

    Doing More: 2 stegosaurus, 6 tricerotops
33. blue, red, red, red
    blue, blue, red, red
    blue, blue, blue, red
    blue, blue, blue, blue
    red, red, red, red

Doing More:
blue, blue, blue, blue
yellow, yellow, yellow, yellow
red, red, red, red
purple, purple, purple, purple
blue, yellow, red, purple
Other solutions are possible.

34 1 quarter, 2 dimes, 4 nickels; or
6 dimes, 1 nickel
Doing More: 3 dimes, 7 nickels

35 4 robots, 3 snakes
Doing More: 2 robots, 6 snakes

36 brown, brown, brown, brown
orange, orange, orange, orange
green, green, green, green
brown, orange, green, green
brown, orange, orange, green
brown, brown, orange, green
Other solutions are possible.

37 35

38 91 cents

39 7 red, 6 purple, 8 yellow, 4 blue

40 48 fudgies, 12 slurpies

41 Bonnie uses 1 quarter and 4 nickels
Rita uses 4 dimes and 1 nickel

42 $4

43 9 orange, 9 yellow, 4 green, 8 blue

44 one $10-bill, two $5-bills, nine $1-bills

45 6 tomatoes, 6 beans, 6 peppers, 6 lettuce; total 24 plants

46 14 ounces

47

48 36 crickets, 63 grasshoppers

49 Anita—monkeys, Lucy—fish, Darrin—snakes, Kwan—birds

50 2 ties, 4 hats

51
4	2	8
3		5
7	6	1

Other solutions are possible.

52 48 hops, 24 jumps

53 48 on ninth day, 53 on tenth day

54 5 stickers, 2 stamps

55 17 blocks long

56
6	7	2
1	5	9
8	3	4

Other solutions are possible.

57 50 people

58 squish, fizz, fire
squish, fire, goo
squish, squish, fizz
squish, fizz, fizz
squish, fire, fire
fizz, fire, goo
fizz, goo, goo
fire, goo, goo

59 45 chickens, 15 geese

60 Bruce—ghost, Clark—robot, Hyru—spider, Helga—cat

61 3 quarters, 7 dimes, 10 nickels, 5 pennies

62 111
113
133
333
555
557
577
777
Other solutions are possible.

63 42 people

64 5 weeks

65 6 quarters, 6 dimes, 12 nickels

66
	Tom	Sara	Dan
1st Row:	Tom	Sara	Dan
2nd Row:	Becka	Andy	Barbara

or

1st Row:	Dan	Sara	Tom
2nd Row:	Barbara	Andy	Becka

67 14 seconds

68 20

Teaching Plan for Story Problem 1

Act out with

The Amazing Money Machine
Cody put one dollar into the Money Machine. The machine whirred and buzzed, then spit out five dollars. "WOW, this is amazing!" he shouted. His friend Nikki put six dollars into the machine, and out came ten dollars. Cody put five dollars in, and out came nine dollars. Then Nikki put ten dollars into the machine. How many dollars came out?

Give students play money and a copy of page 3.

Find Out and Talk About It
- What did Cody do? *He put one dollar into the Money Machine.*
- What did the machine do? *Whirred, buzzed, and spit out five dollars*
- What did Nikki do? *She put six dollars into the machine.* What happened then? *Ten dollars came out.*
- What did Cody do? *Put in five dollars* What happened then? *Nine dollars came out.*
- What did Nikki do then? *Put ten dollars into the machine*
- What do we have to find out to solve this problem? *How many dollars came out of the machine when Nikki put in ten*

Use Strategies
- To help us solve this problem, we can look for a pattern in it. In a pattern, something is repeated again and again.
- Would it help to use play money to act out the story problem and figure out the pattern? *Yes* Acting out a problem with objects is a good way to solve some problems.

Solve It
- When Cody put one dollar into the machine, how many dollars came out? *5*
- When Nikki put in six dollars, how many dollars came out? *10*
- When Cody put in five dollars, how many dollars came out? *9*
- Can we find a pattern in what the machine is doing to the money Cody and Nikki put in? *Yes, the machine adds four dollars to what they put in.*
- Then how many dollars will come out when Nikki puts in ten dollars? *14*

Check It
Read the problem again and have the students check to see if their answer matches the conditions of the problem.

Teaching Plan for Story Problem 2

Look for a Pattern
Act out with ⬜

Give students cubes and a copy of page 4.

> ② **The Pirates**
> Mice have been taking chunks of cheese from the captain's kitchen. They keep stacking the chunks in their kitchen below deck. Each day their stack gets bigger.
>
> Monday   Tuesday   Wednesday   Thursday
>
> If the mice keep using the same pattern, what will the stack look like on Friday?

Find Out and Talk About It
- What have the mice been doing? *Taking chunks of cheese from the captain's kitchen* What have the mice done with the chunks of cheese? *Stacked the chunks in their kitchen*
- What do we know about the stacks of chunks? *They keep getting bigger every day. The mice are using a pattern in the way they stack the chunks.*
- What do we have to find out to solve this problem? *What the stack will look like on Friday if the mice keep using the same pattern*

Use Strategies
- To help us solve this problem, we can look for a pattern, something that is repeated again and again.
- Would it help to use cubes to figure out the pattern? *Yes* Acting out problems with objects is a good way to solve some problems.

Solve It
- How many chunks are there in the stack on Monday? *1* How many on Tuesday? *3* Then how many chunks did the mice add on Tuesday? *2*
- How many chunks are there in the stack on Wednesday? *6* How many chunks did the mice add that day? *3*
- How many chunks are there in the stack on Thursday? *10* How many chunks did the mice add that day? *4*
- Do you see a pattern in the way the mice are adding chunks to their stack? *Each day they add as many as they added the day before, plus one more.* (Students may describe the pattern in many different ways.)
- If the mice keep using that pattern, how many chunks will be in their stack on Friday? *15*

Check It
Read the problem again and have the students check to see if their answer matches the conditions of the problem.

Name _____

Look for a Pattern
Act out with

The Amazing Money Machine

Cody put one dollar into the Money Machine. The machine whirred and buzzed, then spit out five dollars. "WOW, this is amazing!" he shouted. His friend Nikki put six dollars into the machine, and out came ten dollars. Cody put five dollars in, and out came nine dollars. Then Nikki put ten dollars into the machine. How many dollars came out?

Number of dollars _____

Your Turn

Write your own story problem about the amazing money machine. Let a friend solve your problem.

Name _____

Look for a Pattern
Act out with

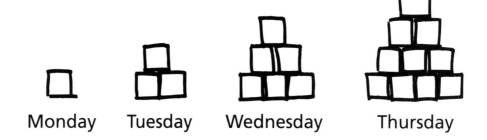

② The Pirates

Mice have been taking chunks of cheese from the captain's kitchen. They keep stacking the chunks in their kitchen below deck. Each day their stack gets bigger.

Monday   Tuesday   Wednesday   Thursday

If the mice keep using the same pattern, what will the stack look like on Friday?

Draw the picture.

Stack on Friday

Doing More

If the mice keep taking cheese in the same way, what will their stack look like on Saturday? What is the pattern? Write about it.

Name _____

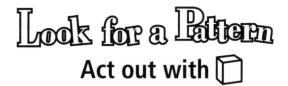

③ Chelsea's Pizza

Kids were lining up to buy Chelsea's cheese pizza. Chelsea and her friend Kris sold 1 slice in the first minute, and 6 slices in the second minute. They sold 11 slices in the third minute, and 16 slices in fourth minute. If the pattern continued, how many slices did they sell in the fifth minute?

Number of slices _____

Doing More

If Chelsea started out with 80 slices of pizza, when did she sell her last slice?

Name _____

Look for a Pattern

Act out with

4 Petfood Plaza

It is Bargain Bonanza Day at Petfood Plaza. Sari pays for 8 bags of Healthy Hamster and gets 16. Vanessa buys 5 boxes of Canary Crunch and gets 10. Bryan buys 7 Dog Toys and gets 14. If Alex buys 9 bags of Nibble Kibble, how many bags will he get?

Number of bags _____

Your Turn

Write your own story problem about Bargain Bonanza Day at Petfood Plaza. Let a friend solve your problem.

Name _____

Look for a Pattern
Act out with

⑤ Mouse Control

Ben is playing a game on the computer. There are 36 mice on the screen. Ben clicks once and 11 mice dash off. He clicks again and 9 mice zip off the screen. When he clicks again, 7 mice vanish.

first click   second click   third click

How many mice will zoom off on Ben's next click? What will the rest of the mice look like on the screen?

Pattern: _____
_____   fourth click

Your Turn

Write your own story problem, using a different pattern. Let a friend solve your problem.

Name _____

Look for a Pattern
Act out with 🎲

Best Seller

Word is getting around that *From Cracks to Crackers* is a perfect book for young ants. Aunt Bee's Bookstore sold 3 copies on Monday, 6 copies on Tuesday, 12 copies on Wednesday, and 24 copies on Thursday. If the pattern continues, how many copies will the bookstore sell on Saturday?

Number of copies _____

Doing More

Aunt Bee's Bookstore started out with 200 copies of the book. How many copies were left when the store closed on Saturday night?

Teaching Plan for Story Problem 7

Act out with ▢

Waveworld
Becky's class went on a special trip to Waveworld. At the park, 17 students went on the Megafoam Ride, 18 students went on the Waterfall, and 10 students went on both rides. How many students were on the trip from Becky's class?

Give students cubes and a copy of page 11.

Find Out and Talk About It
- Where did Becky's class go? *To Waveworld*
- How many students went on the Megafoam Ride? *17* How many students went on the Waterfall Ride? *18* How many students went on both rides? *10*
- What do we have to find out to solve this problem? *How many students were on the trip*

Use Strategies
- To help us solve this problem we can make a Venn circle diagram to show the students on each ride and the students on both rides.
- Would it help to use cubes to represent the students and move them around to show the numbers for each ride? *Yes* Using things, or objects, to act out the problem is a good way to solve some problems.

Solve It
- If we show each ride with a circle, how many circles do we need in our Venn diagram? *2* Are there students who went on both rides? *Yes* Do we need separate or overlapping circles? *Overlapping, to show the students who went on both rides* How should we label the first circle? *Megafoam* How should we label the second circle? *Waterfall*
- Let's put cubes in the Megafoam circle. How many do we need? *17* Where shall we put them in the circle, and do we need to think about the overlapping part of this circle? *10 go in the overlapping part, and then the rest go in the other part of the circle*
- Now how many cubes go in the Waterfall circle? *18* Where do they go? *In the overlapping part and the other part* How many in each part? *There are already 10 in the overlapping part, so the rest of the 18, or 8, go in the other part of the circle.*
- Now how can we find the number of students on the trip? *Add up the cubes in the circles* How many? *25*

Check It
Read the problem again and have the students check to see if their answer matches the conditions in the problem.

Teaching Plan for Story Problem 8

Act out with

Pizza Peppers
Tiffany put pieces of red and green peppers on the pizza. One half of the pieces were red. She put 6 red pieces on the pizza. How many green pieces did she use, and how many pieces all together?

Give students cubes and a copy of page 12.

Find Out and Talk About It
- What is Tiffany doing? *Putting pieces of peppers on the pizza*
- What color are the peppers? *Red and green*
- What do we know about the red peppers? *There are 6 red pieces and they are one half of the total number*
- What do we have to find out to solve this problem? *How many green pieces she used and how many pieces all together*

Use Strategies
- To help us solve this problem we can make a circle and divide it into fractional parts to show how the whole group of pepper pieces is divided.
- Would it help to use cubes to represent the pieces of pepper and move them around to show each half? *Yes* Using things, or objects, to act out the problem is a good way to solve some problems.

Solve It
- If we draw a circle to show the whole group of pepper pieces, how do we want to divide it? *Into halves, or two equal parts*
- If we put the red pieces on one half, how many cubes should we use? *6*
- If the red pieces are one half of the whole, then what do we know about the green pieces? *That they are also one half of the whole group*
- Then how many green pieces are there? *6* How many cubes should we put in the other half of the circle? *6*
- How many pieces of pepper are there in all? *12*

Check It
Read the problem again and have the students check to see if their answer matches the conditions in the problem.

Name _____

Make a Picture or Diagram
Act out with

7. Waveworld

Becky's class went on a special trip to Waveworld. At the park, 17 students went on the Megafoam Ride, 18 students went on the Waterfall, and 10 students went on both rides. How many students were on the trip from Becky's class?

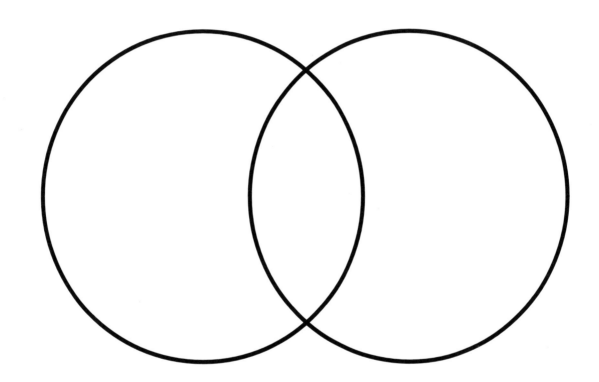

Number of students _____

Doing More

What if 17 students were on the Megafoam ride, 22 students on the Waterfall, and 12 students on both rides. How many students would have been on Becky's trip?

Name _____

Make a Picture or Diagram
Act out with

8. Pizza Peppers

Tiffany put pieces of red and green peppers on the pizza. One half of the pieces were red. She put 6 red pieces on the pizza. How many green pieces did she use, and how many pieces all together?

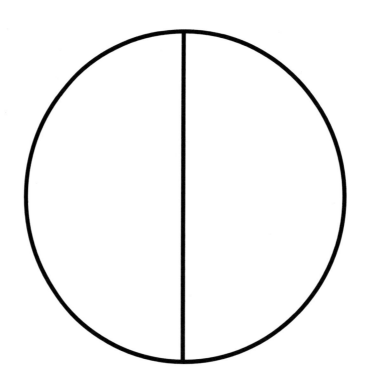

Number of green pieces _____

Total number _____

Doing More

What if Tiffany put 9 red pieces on the pizza. How many pieces would be green? How many pieces would she use in all?

Name _____

Make a Picture or Diagram

Benny the Bike Messenger

Benny, the bike messenger, is delivering letters and packages on Main Street today. He picks up papers at First Bank and peddles 6 blocks north to the end of Main Street. He leaves the papers at City Bank. Then he turns around and bikes 9 blocks south to pick up a package. He turns around and peddles 4 blocks north to deliver his package and pick up another one. He then bikes 9 blocks south to the end of Main Street. How many blocks long is Main Street?

Number of blocks _____

Your Turn

Make up your own story about Benny delivering letters and packages on another street. See if a friend can figure out how long the new street is.

Name _____

Make a Picture or Diagram
Act out with

10 **Danny's Drink Stand**

Saturday was the big race to raise money for the Children's Hospital. Everyone was thirsty after the race and came to Danny's Drink Stand. Then 27 people drank lemonade, 35 people drank water, and 15 people drank both drinks. How many people stopped at Danny's stand?

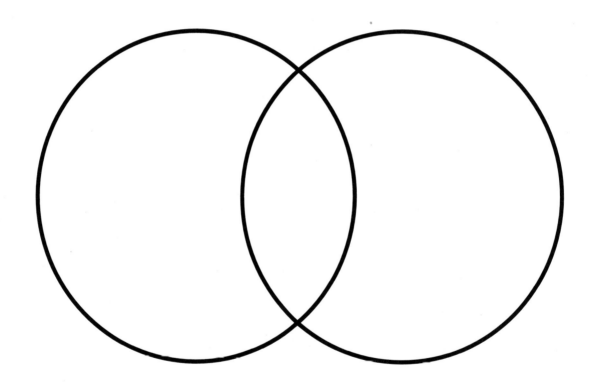

Number of people _____

Doing More

What if 40 people had lemonade, 36 people had water, and 18 people had both drinks, then how many people would have stopped at Danny's Stand?

Name _____

Make a Picture or Diagram
Act out with ▯

Cookie Time

Meg is decorating cookies on a cookie sheet with red, green, and yellow candies. She put each color on the same number of cookies. One third of the cookies have red candies. She put red candies on 10 cookies. How many cookies did Meg decorate?

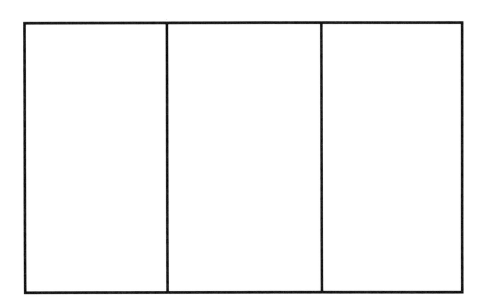

Number of cookies _____

Doing More

What if Meg put red candies on 11 cookies. Then how many cookies did she decorate?

Get Your Hands on Problem Solving, Grade 3 © Ideal

Name _____

Make a Picture or Diagram

Dino's Ferry Service

Dino takes people up and down Moss River in his boat. Today he starts at Jay Landing. He picks up passengers and takes them 1 mile north to Elm Street. Then new people get on his boat and he takes them 6 miles south to the end of Moss River. New people get on and he takes them 4 miles north to Beach Street. He picks up new people and goes south 2 miles to Dusty Cove. He picks up one person here and goes 7 miles north to the end of the river. How long is Moss River?

Draw a picture of the river.

Number of miles _____

Your Turn

Make up your own story about Dino's Ferry Service on another river. See if someone can find out how long the new river is.

Teaching Plan for Story Problem 13

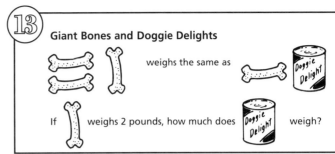

Give students a copy of page 19.

Find Out and Talk About It
- What weighs the same as three Giant Dog Bones? *One Giant Dog Bone and one can of Doggie Delight*
- How much does one Giant Dog Bone weigh? *2 pounds*
- What do we have to find out to solve this problem? *What a can of Doggie Delight weighs*

Use Strategies
- We can use a special kind of thinking, called "logical thinking." We can use this kind of thinking and clues given in the problem to help us solve the problem.

Solve It
- How much does one Giant Dog Bone weigh? *2 pounds*
- Then how much do three bones weigh? *3 x 2 = 6 pounds*
- How much does one dog bone and the can of Doggie Delight weigh together? *6 pounds*
- If you know what a dog bone weighs, and you know what the can and the bone weigh together, then what is a way you can find out what the can of Doggie Delight weighs by itself? *You can subtract 2 pounds from 6 pounds, which is 4 pounds.* How much does the can of Doggie Delight weigh? *4 pounds*

Check It
Read the problem again and have the students check to see if their answer matches the conditions in the problem.

Teaching Plan for Story Problem 14

 Food on the Run

Juan, Rodney, Maria, and Joan ordered snacks at Food on the Run. They ordered an apple, raisins, a popsicle, and a chocolate chip cookie. Juan likes large red pieces of fruit. Maria likes anything with chocolate in it. Joan doesn't like cold snacks. What did each person order?

Give students a copy of page 20.

Find Out and Talk About It

- Where are Juan, Rodney, Maria, and Joan? *At Food on the Run* What are they doing there? *Ordering snacks*
- What did they order? *An apple, raisins, a popsicle, and a chocolate chip cookie*
- What do we know about what Juan likes? *He likes large red pieces of fruit.*
- What do we know about Maria? *She likes anything with chocolate in it.*
- What do we know about Joan? *She doesn't like cold snacks.*
- What do we have to find out to solve this problem? *What food each person ordered*

Use Strategies

- We can use a special kind of thinking, called "logical thinking." We can use this kind of thinking and the clues to help us solve this problem.
- We can also draw a special kind of diagram to help solve this problem. The diagram has four rows for the children and four columns for the snacks.

Solve It

- Let's use the clue about Juan. Use this clue to figure out what he ordered. *The large red piece of fruit would be the apple.* We can write yes under apple for Juan. Then where can we write no? *Under raisins, popsicle, cookie for Juan; and under apple for Rodney, Maria, and Joan*
- What does the clue for Maria tell us? *That she likes chocolate, so she must have ordered the cookie.* We can write yes under cookie for her. Where can we write no? *Under raisins and popsicle for Maria, and under cookie for Rodney and Joan*
- What does the clue about Joan tell us? *That she doesn't like anything cold* What is left that she could have ordered? *Popsicle and raisins* Then what do you think she ordered? *Raisins* Where can we write yes? *Under raisins for Joan* Where can you write no? *Under popsicle for Joan, and raisins for Rodney*
- Now can we figure out what Rodney ordered? *Yes, because there's only one box left without a yes or no in it* What did Rodney order? *The popsicle*

Check It

Read the problem again and have the students check to see if their answer matches the conditions in the problem.

Get Your Hands on Problem Solving, Grade 3 © Ideal

Name _____

Use Logical Thinking

13. Giant Bones and Doggie Delights

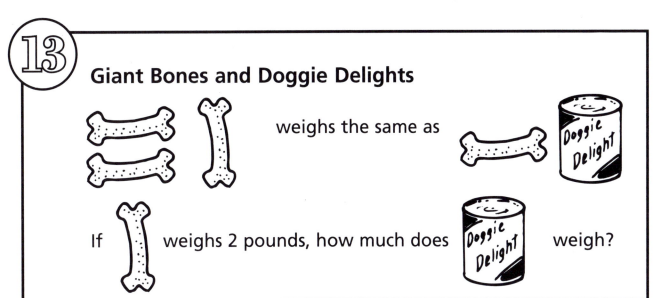

Number of pounds _____

Doing More

What if a Giant Bone weighs 1 pound. Then how much does a can of Doggie Delight weigh?

Name _____

Food on the Run

Juan, Rodney, Maria, and Joan ordered snacks at Food on the Run. They ordered an apple, raisins, a popsicle, and a chocolate chip cookie. Juan likes large red pieces of fruit. Maria likes anything with chocolate in it. Joan doesn't like cold snacks. What did each person order?

	apple	raisins	popsicle	chocolate chip cookie
Juan				
Rodney				
Maria				
Joan				

Juan _____   Rodney _____

Maria _____   Joan _____

Your Turn

Make up your own problem about Juan, Rodney, Maria, and Joan. Give clues about the snacks they order. See if a friend can solve your problem.

Name _____

The Animal Express

Frog, Cat, Bird, and two rabbits are lined up to buy tickets for the Animal Express. A rabbit is first in line. Frog is between a rabbit and Cat. Bird is not next to Cat. Cat is not last in line. How could the animals be lined up?

Show how the animals are lined up.

Your Turn

Now line up the same animals in a different way. Write clues for the way you line them up. Have a friend find your arrangement of animals in line.

Name _____

Use Logical Thinking

16 **Furry Fun Store**

 costs the same as

If costs $6, how much does  cost?

Amount of money _____

Doing More

If the rabbit costs $8, then how much would the bear cost?

Name _____

Use Logical Thinking

Saturday at the Park

Tyrone, Ray, Jamila, and Sandy like to go to the park on Saturday. One likes to swim, one likes to play tennis, another likes to play soccer, and one likes to ride a bike. Tyrone likes the water. Sandy doesn't like to chase balls. Ray doesn't like to use a racquet. What does each one like to do at the park?

	swim	tennis	soccer	bike
Tyrone				
Ray				
Jamila				
Sandy				

Tyrone _____   Ray _____

Jamila _____   Sandy _____

Your Turn

Change the problem. Make up a new set of clues about what everyone likes to do. Can a friend solve your problem?

Name _____

Forest Treats

There are six animals lined up at Forest Treats, waiting for Frog to open the store. There are two bears, two rabbits, Owl, and Chipmunk. One of the bears is first in line. Owl is waiting between two rabbits. A bear is next to last in the line. Where is each animal in the line?

Show where each animal is in the line.

Doing More

Yesterday, there were two frogs, two bears, Owl, and Chipmunk. Owl is first. The frogs are next to each other. A bear is last. Chipmunk is between the two bears. Where is each one in line?

Teaching Plan for Story Problem 19

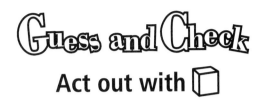

Act out with ⬜

At the Bird Feeder
Wings are flapping and bird seed is flying off in all directions! Leila looks at the bird feeder. She counts 16 birds in all. There are three more red birds than blue birds. There are two fewer yellow birds than blue birds. How many red birds are at the feeder? How many yellow birds? How many blue birds?

Give students cubes and a copy of page 27.

Find Out and Talk About It
- What is Leila doing? *Counting birds at the bird feeder*
- How many birds does she count in all? *16*
- What do we know about the red birds? *There are 3 more than the blue*
- What do we know about the yellow birds? *There are 2 fewer than the blue*
- What do we have to find out to solve this problem? *How many red, yellow, and blue birds there are*

Use Strategies
- To help us solve this problem, we can make guesses and check to see if our guesses are right.
- Would it help to use cubes to make groups of birds and move them around until we have the right number of each color? *Yes* Using things, or objects, to act out the problem is a good way to solve some problems.

Solve It
This is just a sample of the guess-and-check process. Students could begin with many different guesses.
- Let's make a guess about the number of blue birds. *6* If we guess 6 blue birds, then how many red birds would there be? *9* How many yellow birds? *4* How many birds would there be in all? *19*
- That's too many, so let's make another guess for blue birds. *4* If we guess 4 blue, then how many red would there be? *6* How many yellow? *2* How many birds would there be in all? *21*
- That is too low. Let's try again. *5* If we guess 5 blue birds, then how many red birds would there be? *8* How many yellow? *3* How many birds in all? *16*

Check It
Read the problem again and have the students check to see if their answer matches the conditions in the problem.

Teaching Plan for Story Problem 20

Act out with 🔲🔲🔲

Who Feeds the Dog?
Alejandro told his sister Olga that if she solved his puzzle in 5 minutes, he would feed the dog. He drew 8 squares arranged in a square. Then he said, "Use the numbers 1 through 8. Put a different number in each square. The sum of the numbers on each side of the square must be 12." Alejandro fed the dog! What was Olga's answer?

Give students number tiles and a copy of page 28.

Find Out and Talk About It
- What did Alejandro tell his sister? *He would feed the dog if she solved his puzzle in 5 minutes.*
- Then what did he do? *He drew 8 squares arranged in a square.*
- What did he tell Olga to do? *Use the numbers 1 through 8. Put a different number in each square.*
- What else did he say? *That the sum of the numbers on each side must be 12*
- What do we have to find out to solve this problem? *Which number goes in each square*

Use Strategies
- To help us solve this problem, we can make guesses and check to see if our guesses are right.
- Would it help to move the number tiles around on the squares until the sides each show 12? *Yes* Using things, or objects, to act out the problem is a good way to solve some problems.

Solve It
- First let's think of three numbers that add up to 12, then we can try putting these on a side. What three numbers could we use? *8 + 3 + 1 = 12* (This is a sample guess.) Where could we put them? *Across the top, with the 1 in the top right-hand corner and the 3 in the middle*
- What two numbers could we put on the side under 1? *7 and 4, 1 + 7 + 4 = 12*
- Have the students keep moving the tiles around until they find the right combinations of numbers so that each side adds up to 12.

Check It
Read the problem again and have the students check to see if their answer matches the conditions in the problem.

Name _____

Act out with

19   At the Bird Feeder

Wings are flapping and bird seed is flying off in all directions! Leila looks at the bird feeder. She counts 16 birds in all. There are three more red birds than blue birds. There are two fewer yellow birds than blue birds. How many red birds are at the feeder? How many yellow birds? How many blue birds?

Number of red _____ blue _____ yellow _____

Doing More

Another day there were 22 birds at the feeder. There were two more red birds than blue birds, and half as many yellow birds as blue birds. How many birds of each color were at the feeder?

Name _____

Act out with

Who Feeds the Dog?

Alejandro told his sister Olga that if she solved his puzzle in 5 minutes, he would feed the dog. He drew 8 squares arranged in a square. Then he said, "Use the numbers 1 through 8. Put a different number in each square. The sum of the numbers on each side of the square must be 12." Alejandro fed the dog! What was Olga's answer?

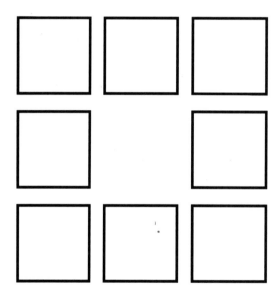

Doing More

Another night Alejandro had a triangle puzzle. Make 6 squares and arrange them in a triangle, with three squares on each side. Use the numbers 1 through 6. Put the numbers in the squares so that each side has a sum of 9.

Name _____

Guess and Check
Act out with

A Bag of Coins

Josh found a bag of coins in the back of his closet. In the bag there were three times as many pennies as nickels, and one half as many dimes as nickels. All together the coins were worth 78 cents. What coins did Josh find?

Number of pennies _____ nickels _____ dimes _____

Doing More

Josh found a second bag. In this bag there were twice as many nickels as pennies, and the same number of nickels and quarters. These coins were worth 61 cents. What were the coins in the second bag?

Name _____

Act out with ▢

Tons of T-shirts

Kendra buys bright-colored T-shirts at garage sales. Now she has 13 of them. She has the same number of blue ones as green ones. She has two more white ones than blue ones. She has three fewer orange shirts than white shirts. How many shirts does Kendra have of each color?

Number of blue _____ green _____ white _____ orange _____

Your Turn

Make up your own problem about Kendra and her T-shirts. Give clues about the number of each color. See if a friend can solve your problem.

Name _____

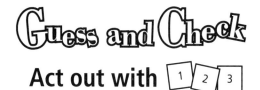

Sixteen on a Side

The twins were entertaining each other with puzzles. Allie gave Tommy a picture and these directions: Take the numbers 2 through 9 and put them in the small squares. The numbers on each side of the large square must add up to 16. Look at the picture below and figure out how Tommy solved the problem.

Doing More

Do the problem again using the numbers 2 through 9. This time make the sum of 18 on each side.

Get Your Hands on Problem Solving, Grade 3 © Ideal

Name _____

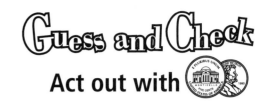

Act out with

Birthday Time

Mamiko had just the right amount of money for her mother's birthday card. She had $1.45 in coins. She had four times as many dimes as quarters. She had one more nickel than quarters. What coins did she have?

Number of quarters _____ dimes _____ nickels _____

Doing More

Mamiko bought a plant for $2.60. She paid the exact amount with coins. She had three times as many dimes as quarters and four fewer nickels than dimes. What coins did she use to pay for the plant?

Teaching Plan for Story Problem 25

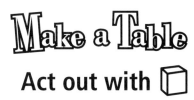

Act out with 🔲

Pampered Pets
The Pampered Pet Shop is giving away Kitty Treats and Doggie Delights today. There are 17 dogs and 3 kittens in the store already. One more dog and one more kitten are coming into the shop every minute. If dogs and kittens keep coming in like that, soon there will be three times as many dogs as kittens in the shop. How many of each will be in the shop then?

Give students cubes and a copy of page 35.

Find Out and Talk About It
- What is the Pampered Pet Shop doing? *Giving away Kitty Treats and Doggie Delights*
- How many dogs are in the store? *17* How many kittens? *3*
- What do we know about the dogs and kittens that are still coming into the shop? *One more dog and one more kitten are coming in every minute.*
- What else do we know about the dogs and kittens? *Soon there will be three times as many dogs as kittens in the shop.*
- What do we have to find out to solve this problem? *How many dogs and how many kittens will be in the shop then*

Use Strategies
- To help us solve this problem, we can make a table to keep track of how many dogs and kittens are in the shop.
- Would it help to use cubes to help us see what is happening in the problem? *Yes* Acting out problems with objects is helpful for solving some problems.

Solve It
- How many kittens are in the shop now? *3* How many dogs are in the shop now? *17*
- How many kittens and dogs will come in each minute? *1 dog and 1 kitten* Then how many kittens will be in the shop after one minute? *4* How many dogs will there be then? *18* Is 18 three times 4? *No*
- How many kittens will be in the shop after two minutes? *5* How many dogs will there be then? *19* Is 19 three times 5? *No*
- Have the children continue filling in the numbers for dogs and kittens after each minute, checking each time to see whether the number of dogs is three times the number of kittens. They will find that after the fourth minute, the number of dogs (21) is three times the number of kittens (7).

Check It
Read the problem again and have the children check to see if their solution matches the conditions of the problem.

Teaching Plan for Story Problem 26

Whales
Wade collects posters, books, and other things about whales. He gets an allowance of $1.75 every week, and he puts it into his savings. After every three weeks, he takes $1.25 out of his savings and spends it on stuff about whales. In how many weeks will he have $9.25 in his savings?

Give students play money and a copy of page 36.

Find Out and Talk About It
- What is Wade doing? *Collecting posters, books, and other things about whales*
- How much money does he get every week for an allowance? *$1.75* What does he do with it? *Puts it in his savings*
- What do we know about how Wade spends his savings money? *Every three weeks he takes $1.25 out of his savings and spends it on stuff about whales.*
- What do we have to find out to solve this problem? *How many weeks it will take him to have $9.25 in his savings*

Use Strategies
- To help us solve this problem, we can make a table to keep track of the money Wade puts into his savings and takes out of it.
- Would it help to use play money to show what is happening in the story problem? *Yes* Acting out story problems with objects can help us solve some problems.

Solve It
- How much money does Wade put into his savings the first week? *$1.75*
- How much does he put into his savings the second week? *$1.75* Then how much money in all does he have in his savings? *$3.50*
- How much does he put into his savings the third week? *$1.75* How much does he take out the third week? *$1.25* Then how much money in all does he have in his savings? *$4.00* (Have students continue filling in the table until they find the solution.)
- In how many weeks will Wade have $9.25 in his savings? *7*

Check It
Read the problem again and have the students check to see if their answer matches the conditions of the problem.

Name _____

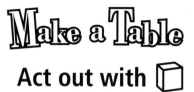

Act out with ▢

25

Pampered Pets

The Pampered Pet Shop is giving away Kitty Treats and Doggie Delights today. There are 17 dogs and 3 kittens in the store already. One more dog and one more kitten are coming into the shop every minute. If dogs and kittens keep coming in like that, soon there will be three times as many dogs as kittens in the shop. How many of each will be in the shop then?

		Minutes							
	Now	1	2	3	4	5	6	7	
Kittens in shop	3	4							
Dogs in shop	17	18							

Number of dogs _____ kittens _____

Doing More

If kittens and dogs keep coming into the shop in the same way, soon there will be two times as many dogs as kittens. How many of each will be in the store then?

Name _____

Make a Table

Act out with

Whales

Wade collects posters, books, and other things about whales. He gets an allowance of $1.75 every week, and he puts it into his savings. After every three weeks, he takes $1.25 out of his savings and spends it on stuff about whales. In how many weeks will he have $9.25 in his savings?

Week	1	2	3	4	5	
Saves (+)	1.75	1.75	1.75			
Spends (-)			1.25			
Total in Savings	1.75	3.50				

Number of weeks _____

Doing More

What if you got an allowance of $2.00 every week, and you spent $1.25 after every third week. How soon would you have over $13 in your savings?

Name _____

Make a Table
Act out with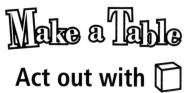

Terrible T-Rex

The third graders are waiting to see "The Terrible Tyrant" at the Dinosaur Museum. The students are in groups of 4, and each group has a grandparent with them. If there are 35 people waiting to see the movie, how many of them are students and how many are grandparents?

Groups	Students	Grandparents	Total People
1	4	1	5
2	8	2	10

Number of students _____ grandparents _____

Doing More

Look for a pattern in the numbers in your table. If there were 50 people in the room, how many of them would be students and how many would be grandparents?

Name _____

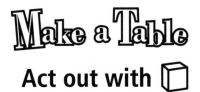

Act out with ▢

Crazy Hats

The Crazy Hats Factory is rushing to get an order of hats out to a store. The workers are packing 5 pig hats and 7 goat hats in each box. If 72 hats have been packed in boxes, how many of each hat did the store order?

Boxes	Pig hats	Goat hats	Total hats
1			
2			

Number of pig hats _____ goat hats _____

Your Turn

Write your own story problem about hats being packed at the Crazy Hats Factory. Let a friend solve your problem.

Name _____

Make a Table

Act out with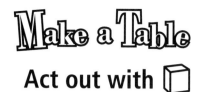

 29

D.J.'s Garden

D.J. loves to grow weird plants in his garden. He planted 18 smuzzywompers and 3 caterpillums. ("Yuk, caterpillums!" says his sister.) D.J. keeps planting 2 more smuzzywompers and 2 more caterpillums until he has twice as many smuzzywompers as caterpillums in his garden. How many of each plant are in D.J.'s garden then?

smuzzywompers	caterpillums
18	3

Number of smuzzywompers _____ caterpillums _____

Doing More

D.J. planted 18 picklefobs and 2 ketchopias. If he keeps planting 1 more of each kind every day, soon there will be three times as many picklefobs as ketchopias. How many will there be of each kind?

Name _____

Make a Table

Act out with

Basketball

Marcie gets $2.00 every week for baby-sitting her little brother. She is saving up money for a basketball. At the end of every four weeks, she takes $1.50 out of her savings and spends it on basketball cards. In how many weeks will she have $16.00 in her savings?

Week	1	2	3	4	5	
Saves (+)						
Spends (-)						
Total in Savings						

Number of weeks _____

Doing More

How many weeks would it take Marcie to save $25?

Teaching Plan for Story Problem 31

Act out with

Cats and Cartoons
Tina loves cats and cartoons. At a garage sale one day, she saw a book of cat cartoons that cost 20 cents. Tina quickly reached into her pocket and took out 8 coins. What coins did she use to buy the book?

Give students play money and a copy of page 43.

Find Out and Talk About It
- What was Tina doing? *She was looking at a book of cat cartoons at a garage sale.*
- How much did the book cost? *20 cents*
- How many coins did Tina use to pay for the book? *8*
- What do we have to find out to solve this problem? *What coins Tina used*

Use Strategies
- To help us solve this problem, we can make an organized list. Making this kind of step-by-step list helps us keep track of all the combinations of coins that are worth 20 cents. It also makes it easy for us to see that we have found **all** of the combinations.
- Would it help to use play coins to find all the combinations? *Yes* Acting out problems with objects is a good way to solve some problems.

Solve It
- One way to solve this problem in an organized way is to start with the group of fewest coins that are worth 20 cents, 2 dimes. (Let students know that there are other ways, as well, to solve the problem in an organized way.) We can record 2 dimes, zero nickels, and zero pennies. How many coins in all? *2*
- We can change 1 dime for 2 nickels. Now how many coins in all? *3*
- If we change 1 nickel for 5 pennies, then how many dimes do we have? *1* How many nickels? *1* How many pennies? *5* How many coins in all? *7*
- If we change the other nickel for pennies, how many dimes do we have? *1* How many nickels? *0* How many pennies? *10* How many coins in all? *11*
- Have the students continue trading coins for other coins and filling in the list until they have found all possible combinations. Then have them look for the combination of 8 coins. You may want to point out that there is often more than one solution for this kind of problem.
- What coins did Tina use? *3 nickels and 5 pennies*

Check It
Read the problem again and have the students check to see if their answer matches the conditions of the problem.

Teaching Plan for Story Problem 32

Act out with

Dino-Mite Sale!
The Museum Shop had a sale on toy dinosaurs. Each stegosaurus cost 4 cents and each triceratops cost 5 cents. Jamie bought 8 of the dinosaurs and paid 34 cents. How many of each kind did Jamie get?

Give students play money and a copy of page 44.

Find Out and Talk About It
- What was happening at the Museum Shop? *A sale on toy dinosaurs*
- How much did a stegosaurus cost? *4 cents* How much did a triceratops cost? *5 cents*
- How many dinosaurs did Jamie buy? *8* How much did he pay? *34 cents*.
- What do we have to find out to solve this problem? *How many of each kind Jamie got*

Use Strategies
- To help us solve this problem, we can make an organized list. It will help us keep track of how much different numbers of dinos would cost. Then we can find the combination of 8 dinos that would cost 34 cents.
- Would it help to use play coins to find all the groups? *Yes* Acting out story problems with objects is a good way to solve some problems.

Solve It
- How much would 1 stegosaurus cost? *4 cents* How much would 2 cost? *8 cents* (Have the students fill in the rest of the list)
- How much would 1 triceratops cost? *5 cents* How much would 2 cost? *10 cents* (Have the students fill in the rest of the list.)
- Let's start by finding combinations of groups that make 8 dinosaurs in all. If we begin with 1 stegosaurus, how many triceratops would we need? *7* How much would the stegosaurus cost? *4 cents* The triceratops? *35 cents* Does 4 cents and 35 cents equal 34 cents? *No*
- Let's find another combination that makes 8 dinosaurs in all. (Have the students continue in the same way until they find the combination of two groups that total 8 dinos and costs 34 cents.)
- How many dinos of each kind did Jamie get? *6 stegosaurus and 2 triceratops; 24¢ + 10¢ = 34¢*

Check It
Read the problem again and have the children check to see if every possible group of coins is in their list, and if they match the conditions of the problem.

Name _____

Make an Organized List
Act out with

Cats and Cartoons

Tina loves cats and cartoons. At a garage sale one day, she saw a book of cat cartoons that cost 20 cents. Tina quickly reached into her pocket and took out 8 coins. What coins did she use to buy the book?

Groups of coins worth 20 cents

Dimes	Nickels	Pennies	Coins in all

Number of dimes _____ nickels _____ pennies _____

Doing More

What 12 coins could Tina have used to pay for the book?

Get Your Hands on Problem Solving, Grade 3 © Ideal

Name _____

Make an Organized List

Act out with

32 Dino-Mite Sale!

The Museum Shop had a sale on toy dinosaurs. Each stegosaurus cost 4 cents and each triceratops cost 5 cents. Jamie bought 8 of the dinosaurs and paid 34 cents. How many of each kind did Jamie get?

Number of stegosaurus	Pay	Number of triceratops	Pay
1	4¢	1	5¢
2	8¢	2	
3		3	
4		4	
5		5	
6		6	
7		7	
8		8	

Number of stegosaurus _____ triceratops _____

Doing More

If Jamie had paid 38 cents for 8 dinosaurs, how many of each kind would have been in the bag?

44

Get Your Hands on Problem Solving, Grade 3 © Ideal

Name _____

Make an Organized List

Act out with

33 Leaping Fish

The Leaping Fish Shop has 10 neon-blue fish and 10 fire-red fish for sale. The fish are in small closed tanks. Toby, the owner, put a group of 4 fish in each tank. Every group of fish is different. What colors are the fish in each tank?

Colors of fish in tanks

blue, red, red, red
_____
_____
_____
_____
_____

Doing More

Now the shop has 5 neon-blue, 5 fire-red, 5 yellow, and 5 purple fish. There is a group of 4 fish in each tank, and every group is different. What colors could the fish be in each tank?

45

Get Your Hands on Problem Solving, Grade 3 © Ideal

Name _____ Make an Organized List

Act out with

 Tunnel of Terrors

Steve and Donte are buying tickets for a ride through the Tunnel of Terrors. Tickets cost 65 cents. Steve paid for his ticket with 7 coins. He did not use any pennies or half dollars. What coins did he use?

Groups of coins worth _____

Quarters	Dimes	Nickels	Coins in all

Number of quarters _____ nickels _____ dimes _____

Doing More

Donte paid for his ticket with 10 coins. He used only nickels and dimes. What coins did Donte use?

Name _____

Make an Organized List

Act out with

35 Used Goodies

The third graders decided to sell their old toys and books to make money for their trip to the beach. They brought their old things to the school fair. Angela marked each of her toy robots 15 cents. Jordan marked each of his books about snakes 10 cents. Aaron bought 7 of Angela's and Jordan's things for sale and paid 90 cents. How many of each kind did Aaron get?

Number of toy robots	Pay	Number of books about snakes	Pay
1		1	
2		2	
3		3	
4		4	
5		5	
6		6	
7		7	
8		8	

Number of robots _____ snakes _____

Doing More

If Aaron had paid 90 cents for 8 things, how many robots and how many books would he have bought?

Name _____

Make an Organized List

Act out with

36. Big Bug Birthday Party

It's time for the Big Bug Birthday Party. There are 8 brown bugs, 8 orange bugs, and 8 green bugs at the family party. There are 4 bugs at each table. Grandfather Bug looks around and sees that the groups of bugs at every table are different. What colors are the bugs at each table?

Colors of bugs at tables

_____

_____

_____

_____

_____

Doing More

Write your own story problem about a Bug family party. Include 6 bugs each of 4 different colors. Let a friend solve your problem.

Name _____

Vacation Time!

Kareem and Katie did a survey. They asked kids whether they liked to bike or skate during spring vacation. They found out that 23 liked to bike and 28 liked to skate. There were 16 who liked to bike and skate. How many kids took part in their survey?

Number of kids _____

Name _____

For a Change

Alexander bought chips at McNoodle's Market. He was supposed to get 25¢ change, but Mr. McNoodle smiled and gave him 75¢. Amanda bought a muffin. She was supposed to get 12¢ change, but Mr. McNoodle gave her 62¢. Bruno bought a taco. He was supposed to get 35¢ change, but Mr. NcNoodle gave him 85¢. If you were supposed to get 41¢ change, how much would you get back at McNoodle's Market?

Amount of change _____

Name _____

Bright Beads

Violeta and Cindy are making jewelry. They have a bowl of bright-colored beads in front of them. They have 25 beads in all. There are two more yellow beads than purple beads. There are half as many blue beads as yellow beads. There are three more red beads than blue beads. How many beads do they have of each color?

Number of yellow _____ purple _____ blue _____ red _____

Name _____

What's for Lunch?

The third graders went to the cafeteria for lunch. They could choose chocolate fudgies or lemon slurpies. Out of 10 students at each lunch table, 8 chose fudgies and 2 chose slurpies. If 60 third graders ate lunch, how many had fudgies and how many had slurpies?

Number of fudgies _____ slurpies _____

Name _____

The Salamanders Set Sail

Bonnie and Rita are buying tickets to see "The Salamanders Set Sail." Each ticket costs 45 cents. Both of them pay for their ticket with 5 coins. Bonnie uses a quarter, but Rita does not. What coins do the two girls use?

Bonnie's coins _____

Rita's coins _____

Name _____

Fun Time Park Tickets

 costs the same as

If  costs $2, how much does cost?

Cost of 1 Mountain Turn Ticket _____

Name _____

Underwater

Katja and Joe are snorkeling where there are lots of beautiful fish. They saw 30 fish in just a few minutes. They counted the same number of orange fish as yellow fish. They saw twice as many blue fish as green fish. There were five fewer green fish than yellow fish. How many fish of each color did they see?

Number of orange _____ yellow _____ blue _____ green _____

- -

Name _____

A Dozen Bills

Ryan has been saving up his dollars for a football. At the Giant Sports Show, he saw a soccer ball and a football for sale together for $29.00. Ryan took 12 bills out of his pocket and paid for the balls. What bills did he use?

Number of $20 bills ____ $10 bills ____ $5 bills ____ $1 bills ____

Name _____

Veggies

Nellie and Nick are planting tomatoes, beans, peppers, and lettuce in their garden. One fourth of the plants are tomatoes, one fourth are beans, one fourth are peppers, and one fourth are lettuce. They planted 6 tomato plants. How many plants or each kind did they put in their garden, and how many plants in all?

Number of tomatoes _____ beans _____ peppers _____ lettuce _____

Total number _____

Name _____

Cars and Boats

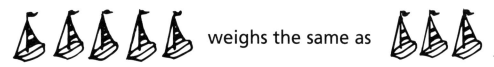 weighs the same as

If 🛥 weighs 7 ounces, how much does  weigh?

Train car _____ ounces

Name _____

 Pig's Picture Gallery

What do you think the next picture will look like?
Draw it.

Name _____

 Leap-off

Teams of crickets and grasshoppers are getting ready for the great Leap-off. The first team is at the starting line. There are 4 crickets and 7 grasshoppers on each team. The whistle blows and the bugs leap off! The Leap-off ends after 99 bugs have leaped. How many of the bugs were crickets and how many were grasshoppers?

Number of crickets _____   grasshoppers _____

Name _____

Zoo Time

Anita, Lucy, Darrin, and Kwan each have their favorite spot at the zoo. Their favorite places include the Snake Room, the Bird Barn, the Fish Place, and the Monkey House. Anita likes to watch animals swing from trees. Darrin likes animals that crawl along the ground. Lucy likes animals that live in water. Which is each person's favorite part of the zoo?

Anita _____

Darrin _____

Lucy _____

Kwan _____

Name _____

Fine Frog-Wear

Frog wanted to look his finest for the Princess, so he went to Fine Frog-Wear to buy a tie and hat. At Fine Frog-Wear, each tie costs 25 cents and each hat costs 50 cents. Frog bought 6 pieces of frog-wear and paid $2.50. How many ties and how many hats did Frog buy?

Number of ties _____ hats _____

Name _____

Rainy Day Puzzles

It's a rainy day and Faruk is making up number puzzles for his sister. Faruk shows her a diagram of squares and says, "OK, here's a hard one! Take the numbers 1 through 8 and put them in these squares so that the sum of the numbers on each side of the larger square is 14." Look at Faruk's diagram and try to solve his problem.

Name _____

Jack Be Nimble

Jack is getting ready for the big Candlestick Jump. He has done 30 one-leg hops already and 6 jumps. He keeps doing 3 hops, then 3 jumps, then 3 hops, 3 jumps, and so on. He stops when he has done twice as many hops as jumps. How many hops and how many jumps has he done?

Number of hops _____ jumps _____

Name _____

Dr. Drummer's Beetles

Dr. Drummer is looking for rare Dancer Beetles along the banks of the river. Here is her record:

Day	1	2	3	4	5	6	7	8
Beetles	8	13	18	23	28	33	38	43

How many beetles will she probably see on the ninth and tenth days?

Number on ninth day _____ tenth day _____

Name _____

Stickers-N-Stamps

The Stickers-N-Stamps Shop carries all kinds of stickers and rubber stamps. Lots of the stickers and stamps have animal pictures on them. Stickers cost 15 cents each and stamps are $1.25 each. Today Jessica bought 7 lion pictures and paid $3.25. How many stickers and how many stamps did she buy?

Number of stickers _____ stamps _____

Name _____

The Craft Fair

Anna and Staci are at the Green Street Craft Fair. They begin at Tammy's T-shirts. Then they go 5 blocks north to the Bead Barn. Next they go 10 blocks south to the end of Green Street and get a smoothie. Next they walk 12 blocks north and stop to watch the clowns. Then they go south for 4 blocks to see the puppet show. When they go 9 blocks to the north end of Green Street, they've seen everything! How many blocks long is Green Street?

Number of blocks _____

Name _____

Marvin's Cheese Closet

Marvin Mouse put a new lock on his cheese closet. The lock has 9 buttons on it, and each one has a number on it. The numbers 1, 2, 3, 4, 5, 6, 7, and 8 are on the buttons. Marvin can push the 3 buttons in any row across, or down, or on a diagonal, to get his secret sum of 15. THAT opens the closet! What number is on each button?

Name _____

The Soccer Players

The city soccer team played every night this week. On Monday, 125 people came to see the game. On Tuesday, 120 people came, and on Wednesday there were 110 people. On Thursday, 95 people came to the game, and on Friday, 75 people came. If the pattern continued, how many people came to the game on Saturday?

Number of people _____

Name _____

Gooey Gumballs

The Gooey Gumball Factory makes the gooiest, best-tasting gumballs in the world. Today the factory made pink squish, chocolate fizz, cherry fire, and green goo gumballs. Your job is to take 6 of each kind and put them in bags of 3, and make every bag different. What 3 gumballs could you put in each bag?

Show the gumballs in each bag.

Name _____

Farmer Luke's Birds

Farmer Luke put the last goose into the back of the truck. He had started with 40 chickens and 10 geese in the truck. Then he kept adding 1 chicken, then 1 goose, then 1 chicken, and 1 goose, and so on, until the truck was full. "There are three times as many chickens as geese in here," he said. "Let's go!" How many chickens and how many geese are in his truck now?

Number of chickens _____ geese _____

Name _____

Trick or Treat

Bruce, Clark, Hyru, and Helga chose their Halloween costumes: a cat, a robot, a spider, and a ghost. They will march in the Ghostly Parade and go trick-or-treating together. Helga's costume has a tail. Bruce's costume is all white. Clark's costume has fewer than 8 legs. Which costume did each person choose?

Bruce _____

Hyru _____

Clark _____

Helga _____

Name _____

Dunk the Teacher

At the school fair, each ticket for "Dunk the Teacher" is $2. For $2 you get three balls to throw at the target. If you hit the target, the teacher goes into a pail of cold water! Glenda takes coins out of her pocket to pay for a ticket. She has twice as many nickels as pennies. She has 3 fewer dimes than nickels. She has 4 more dimes than quarters. What coins does she use?

Number of quarters ____ dimes ____ nickels ____ pennies ____

Name _____

Numba

In the wee town of Numba, there are eight houses. The wee Numba folk start out with six of each of these numbers: 1, 3, 5, and 7. They put the numbers together in groups of three to make house numbers. What are eight different house numbers that the Numba folk could make?

Name _____

Ice Cream Fair

Ben and Terry have a table at the Ice Cream Fair. Their sign says Old Favorites: Chocolate, Vanilla, and Strawberry. This morning they sold 18 cups of chocolate, 24 cups of vanilla, and 12 cups of strawberry. They had 8 people who took both chocolate and vanilla and 4 people who took both vanilla and strawberry. How many people bought cups of ice cream from Ben and Terry?

Number of people _____

Name _____

The Book Club Kids

The Book Club Kids love to read scary chapter books! There are 8 kids in the club, and they each put 75¢ into the club's bank every week. After every two weeks, they take $5.00 out of their bank and buy a new paperback book. How many weeks will it take the club to save up $20.00?

Number of weeks _____

Name _____

Barry's Burgers

Andrea is paying $2.70 for her lunch at Barry's Burgers. She has the exact amount in coins. She has the same number of quarters as dimes. She has twice as many nickels as dimes. What coins does Andrea have?

Number of quarters _____ dimes _____ nickels _____

Name _____

Watching the Game

Sara, Andy, Tom, Dan, and the twins, Becka and Barbara, are watching the volleyball game. They are sitting in two rows, with three in each row. Andy is sitting between the twins. Andy is sitting behind Sara. Dan is not sitting in front of Becka. Where could they be sitting at the game?

Show where each of them is sitting.

Name _____

Ants, Beware!

Julie is playing "Ants, Beware!" on the computer. Six ants march onto the screen every second. As the ants keep coming, a tally number shows the total number of ants on the screen. As soon as the tally number has an 8 in it, a lizard snatches away 8 ants! How many seconds will Julie have to play the game to get 50 ants on the screen?

Number of seconds _____

Name _____

A Ghostly Night

Dana and Olga are getting ready for Halloween. They are hanging up ghosts, skeletons, and monsters in the yard. One half of the things they hang up are ghosts. One fourth of the things are monsters. The rest are skeletons. They hung up 5 monsters. How many scary things did they hang up?

Number of scary things _____